CCSS Genre Fairy Tale

Essential Question
How do we get what we need?

A Gift for Mario

A Mexican Fairy Tale

retold by Chris Ericsson ★ illustrated by Alida Massari

Chapter 1
Javier's Plan 2

Chapter 2
The Tatema 6

Chapter 3
Javier's Trick 9

Chapter 4
Javier Learns a Lesson 12

Respond to Reading. 16

PAIRED READ The Golden Land 17

Focus on Genre. 20

Chapter 1
Javier's Plan

Long ago, in a small village, there lived two friends named Javier and Mario. Javier owned a store and worked extremely hard. He got up early every single morning of the week and worked from dawn to dusk in his store.

Javier's friend Mario didn't get up early. In fact, every day he lay in bed till nearly midday. Then he sent his wife, Hermila, to Javier's store to get coffee and tortillas for his breakfast. Javier never asked Mario to pay for the groceries Hermila collected, but he was getting annoyed with him.

One day, Javier thought to himself, "Why should I work so hard all the time when Mario never works at all and gets everything for nothing?"

All day, Javier brooded about Mario. That night, he decided that from then on, Mario would have to pay for his groceries.

The next day, when Hermila came to the store to fetch Mario's breakfast, Javier said, "I'm sorry, Hermila, but I can no longer give you food and other groceries without payment. My family is growing, and my house is much too small. However, I cannot afford a bigger house. From now on, I need to care for my own family first."

Hermila's face dropped. "But Javier," she said, "you know we have no money."

"I do know that," admitted Javier, "but I have a solution. As I said, my house is too small. I need to add another room. Mario and I can run a barter system. He can help me build another room in exchange for groceries."

Hermila ran home to tell Mario about Javier's plan. She found him having a nap in the sun.

Mario considered what Hermila had told him. "That sounds like a good idea to me," he said. "I'll go and talk to Javier later."

In spite of appearances, Mario was not a lazy man. He was a humble man who strongly believed that he had no right to anything unless it was given to him. Mario did not want great riches or to be a wealthy man. He thought that if he was meant to have something, it would come to him.

Mario would tell his wife, "If we are meant to have money, it will appear at the door."

Chapter 2
The Tatema

Later that day, Mario was wandering through the countryside when he heard someone shouting, "Stop! Stop!"

Mario turned and saw a man trying desperately to halt his runaway horse. Mario did not hesitate. Without a thought for his own safety, he rushed forward, grabbed the horse's bridle, and pulled the horse to a halt.

The rider was a man with a magnificent long white beard. He was full of praise for Mario. Although Mario had never seen the man before, the man seemed to know him.

"You are very brave, Mario," he declared. "You don't waste your energy dashing about all day, but you act quickly and decisively when it is necessary. I want to reward you for saving me from an accident."

"No, no!" cried Mario. "I only did what anyone would have done."

"Very few people would risk their life like that, Mario. Come with me. I want to give you a very special gift—a tatema. Only the person who is given the tatema can keep it."

Mario reluctantly followed the man to an ancient oak tree. He was told that the tatema was buried in the leaves under the tree.

Mario dug through the leaves and was astonished to find two treasure chests. One was filled with silver coins and objects, and the other was filled with gold coins and objects. He turned to thank the man only to discover that both the man and the horse had disappeared.

Mario put a handful of the coins into his pocket and set off home. When he got home, he gave the coins to a disbelieving Hermila, who at once demanded to know where he got them.

"Take the money to Javier's store and buy some food. Ask Javier to come back with you, and I'll tell you both an incredible story," said Mario.

Chapter 3

Javier's Trick

When Mario had finished his tale, Hermila and Javier looked at him in amazement. If they hadn't seen the coins with their own eyes, neither of them would have believed Mario.

"Why didn't you bring the treasure chests home?" asked Javier.

"They were much too heavy to carry—and anyway, if I am meant to have money, it will come to me," replied Mario.

"You can use my mule to collect your treasure chests," said Javier, "in exchange for half the treasure."

"That sounds fair," said Mario.

"We will go at midnight, when everyone in the village is asleep," said Javier. "It'll be better if no one else knows what we are doing."

Javier went back to his store, but for the rest of the day he kept thinking about Mario's treasure.

"Why should I share the treasure with Mario?" he thought. "Mario has no mule, and he would never even have fetched the treasure if I hadn't offered to lend him my mule. If I had all the treasure, I could build a bigger house for my family, and I wouldn't have to work so hard."

At midnight, Hermila woke Mario.

"Javier has not come," she said.

"Never mind," said Mario, yawning. "He must have changed his mind." Then Mario turned over and went back to sleep.

Javier had changed his mind—but only about sharing the treasure with Mario. He had decided to keep it all for himself.

At midnight, Javier led his mule to the tree Mario had described. He dug among the leaves until he found the treasure chests. Javier excitedly opened the first chest, only to find it was filled with mud. The second chest was the same. He scrabbled in the mud, hoping to find some coins, but there was nothing but mud.

Javier was angry. He thought Mario had played a trick on him, and he decided to get revenge on Mario. He loaded the treasure chests onto his mule and took them back to the village. He dumped one chest outside Mario's door, and the other outside Mario's window.

Chapter 4

Javier Learns a Lesson

In the morning, Hermila got up and went to open the door. It wouldn't budge. Then she tried to open the window, but it wouldn't budge, either. Hermila called Mario to help her.

Mario pushed and shoved at the window. It finally opened, and silver coins spilled into the room. Then Mario tried to open the door. After much effort, he opened it a crack, and gold coins flooded the doorway.

"Javier is a good friend," said Mario. "He fetched my treasure all alone."

Later that morning, Hermila took a bag of coins to Javier's store. She gathered up food and other groceries. When Javier opened his mouth to ask Hermila how she planned to pay for the goods, she emptied the bag onto the counter.

"I have come to pay our debt," she said. "You are a good man, Javier. Not only did you travel into the countryside alone at night to fetch the chests, but you did not take your half of the treasure."

"It wasn't me," spluttered Javier, unwilling to admit that he had planned to play a trick on Mario.

"You mustn't deny your kindness," smiled Hermila. "How else could the chests have gotten to our house? No one else knew about them."

Javier looked at Hermila and said quietly, "As Mario has said, if you are meant to have something, it will appear at your door."

Summarize

Use details from the story to summarize *A Gift for Mario*. Your chart may help you.

Details

↓

Point of View

Text Evidence

1. How can you tell this story is a fairy tale? Identify one feature that tells you this. GENRE

2. What can you tell about Mario from the reaction he has after he is rewarded for stopping the runaway horse? POINT OF VIEW

3. What does the word *disbelieving* on page 8 mean? How can the root word *belief* help you figure out the meaning? ROOT WORDS

4. Write about how Mario feels about the treasure and compare it to how Javier feels about the treasure. WRITE ABOUT READING

Compare Texts
Read about the importance of gold.

The Golden Land

Gold was one of the first metals to be discovered, and people have valued it ever since. The search for gold has motivated explorers and adventurers. Gold miners have risked their lives for it, and battles have been fought for it.

It was the lure of gold that led to the conquest of Central and South America by the Europeans. When the explorer Christopher Columbus sailed from Spain in 1492, he was looking for a quick ocean route to Asia. Instead of finding that, Columbus found the New World. He also discovered the abundance of gold there.

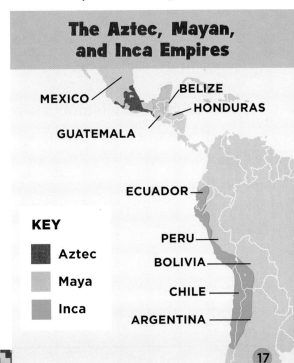

The Aztec, Mayan, and Inca Empires

MEXICO
BELIZE
HONDURAS
GUATEMALA
ECUADOR
PERU
BOLIVIA
CHILE
ARGENTINA

KEY
- Aztec
- Maya
- Inca

Mountain High Maps/Digital Wisdom

Uses for Gold

Aztecs	Mayans	Incas
• clothing decoration • jewelry • protective vests for soldiers	• jewelry • ornamentation for rulers	• religious ceremonies • sandals • jewelry

Although gold was valued by the civilizations of South and Central America, it was not as precious to them as it was to the people of Europe. In fact, the Aztecs of Mexico valued turquoise and feathers more highly than gold. However, the Aztecs, the Incas of South America, and the Mayans of Central America all created beautiful objects from gold, including masks and jewelry.

The voyage of Columbus opened the doors for the conquistadors. These were Spanish soldiers who came to the New World for two main reasons. They wanted to become famous by conquering new lands for Spain. They also wanted gold, and the New World seemed to have plenty of it. Myths about a land where gold was as common as soil encouraged the conquistadors to make their way inland from the coast in the hope of finding this place.

When the Spanish soldiers invaded the Aztec Empire in 1519, the Aztecs welcomed them with gifts of gold. They hoped that the soldiers would be so pleased with the gold that they would go home. However, it just made the soldiers greedy for more.

The Aztecs made beautiful gold jewelry, such as this ring.

When the Spanish defeated the Incas in 1527, the leader of the Spanish troops asked for a huge amount of gold and silver as the ransom for the Inca ruler's freedom. The Incas paid the ransom, and shiploads of gold and other treasure were taken back to Spain.

The diseases brought by the Spanish killed more people in Central and South America than the Spanish themselves did. Essentially, however, it was the European hunger for gold that led to the fall of the Inca and Aztec empires.

Make Connections

Why do people want gold? ESSENTIAL QUESTION

What do *A Gift for Mario* and *The Golden Land* tell you about wealth? TEXT TO TEXT

Kenneth Garrett/National Geographic Society/CORBIS

Focus on

Genre

Fairy Tales Fairy tales are fantasy stories. They are not realistic and can include magical events. Fairy tales are often retold by different authors.

Read and Find *A Gift for Mario* is about a man who is rewarded for a good deed by a magical person. It has the characteristics of a fairy tale. It is not realistic, and it includes magical events. Fairy tales are often very old stories. The storyteller has retold the story in his own words.

Your Turn

Imagine if you were Mario. How would you feel about the tatema? Retell the story as if it were happening to you.